VEHEMENCE

AN ODE TO LUCIDITY

MRINAL YADAV

Made with ♥ on the Notion Press Platform
www.notionpress.com

To,

My parents, who ingrained in me the belief that nothing is impossible and taught me to dream with open eyes.

Contents

Acknowledgements

Every line that we quote is based on our experiences. Experiences that we feel with the people around us. We also contemplate these experiences. Henceforth, these people around us are credible to the vote of thanks. I would like to thank my dear friends for always supporting me through the thick and thin times of mine and some unsaid dear ones who were part of this beautiful journey.

Chrysalis

Doomed for someone and boon for someone
Deep down, Chrysalis is what we all desire for
The present is never great for anyone
An entitled future is what we all aspire for

The caterpillar losing it identity to the four-winged butterfly
The hope of becoming better is always an unprecedented lie
The ability to fly comes at the cost of never being able to crawl again
The happiness of the present is always shadowed by a nostalgic pain

I'm a traveler of the realm of darkness
But the notion of light still fascinates me
Despite being succumbed by the evil madness
The thought of the universal good still elates me

Romance is human's daily bread
The string of attachments isn't just a mere thread
Roses, dandelions, and the letters of the past that shred
The color of love is nothing but red

The steps taken today pave the pathway for the forthcoming
How can life always be so stunning
The spark of hope can turn into illumination for the world ahead

The Future is the sink where every small action of today is fed

I can still hear the cries from past
To the eternity they might last
A hole in the heart that can be felt but not seen
With each passing moment, the gloomy regrets expand their reign

Who are you and who am I?
There's a sense of unity that we can't deny
Leaving behind the contiguous biased minds
Let's celebrate the festivity until the calendar finds

Thoughts getting deeper in the private havens
Connecting to a post line where God sends ravens
Solitude is where good and evil transfuse
Leaving the soul with the decision to choose

White, Grey & Black

It all starts as one of the fairytales
Sadness is not a companion of the night
The epitome of happiness it hails
Childhood is when everything seems white

Then we start doing what is not to be done as per se
Subtly with our pure white thoughts, we part ways
Like a caudate leaving the sea for a short stay
This is the time when everything starts turning gray

The story of yours starts turning into a ho-hum script
Your mind starts finding you in an endless conflict
Then you regret everything, want it intact, want it back
But it took you longer to realize that everything has turned black

Bad Fortune or Bad Life

I try to fix pieces but everything falls apart
The outcomes are always the same, loads of tears and a broken heart
Everyone has a shoulder to cry upon
I lie in a dark room sad and alone

I wish I could have something like them
Like a tree supported by the stem
But alas, it was never my reality
All I gained was a notion of individuality

I wish all of this could stop at this very moment
But there are commitments that I can't evade
Life stares at me, waiting for my happiness to fade
Playing a game that was never supposed to be played

I don't know what my mistakes are?
Maybe my skills of living were not at par
It was all started alone and it will all end alone
I write it in with a trenching heart and a trembling tone

A Candid Confession

If I write about you, I can't
It's not that I don't want
Let me give it a try
I promise I ain't gonna lie

It all started at a random time
In my dark sky, I for once saw a sunshine
We talked about writing, music, and life
You were someone of my type

We weren't frequent but consistent
Somewhere everytime, we were persistent
You had some of the most beautiful ideologies
Due to our coherent vibes, envious were the stars of astrology

From the very first jiff when I saw you
I have been in awe of you
Each moment these days keeps me reminding of you
Deep down inside, I've gained a liking for you

I don't know if you feel the same
I don't know if we are gonna end up in the frame
I promise I won't let you down

You're one of my most favorite things in the town

Stalls of Happenings

Wandering through the stalls of happenings
Not stopping at each one to reach one
Having an idea of when it'll all be done
The hopes of a better forthcoming beautifully obscure the endings

The downtown alleys, narrow, steep, and occasionally dilapidated
It's hard to get an idea of a change in the landscape if not visited
But still being in excitement, you linger on
To find a place to stop upon

The serene nature never lets you down
At that moment, you cannot frown
It makes you feel like a king without a crown
But the evil time never takes a pause

Was it a random outing or life I was talking about?
That's when I take a stop and read it again to find out
Now I can hear the lines giving the secretive shout
Losing the wordplay, smiling blue, I sigh out

The Grief of Past

Ever got stranded upon, staring at nothing
Glancing at just a bunch of idle objects and still knowing everything
Thinking about every moment that was spent
From the very start to the very end

Dose off eyes and lay back
The dopamine for living that we lack
Was it all ever good?
The instances when you think "whether I should?"

The fall that was never expected
Every passing moment, it makes me feel dejected
The optimistic credence and hope, all scattered and shattered on the ground
As if all was lost and nothing was found

Is there a notion of not trusting again?
A happy life, it would be, with somewhat less pain
We trust people again and again with a belief
But eventually the result is only grief

Mis Amigos

The friends who taught me to live life
The staunch enemies of my mental rife
If breathing could be less essential than something, that would be them
If my life is less precious than something, it would be them

There may be empty pockets, but their hearts are always filled
Such spontaneously is the notion of trust instilled
They are people who are all gray but in a right way
Influencing everything of yours night and day

A life without these idiots is a bad life
Every right talk of theirs, I falsely condemn
Emotions linger for long, and words fall short when I describe them
They are the sine qua non of my sustainable afterlife

The Dry Ecstasy

The green herbs, the white profane
An escape from the reality
A pathway where everything is insane
Or so does it seem when you stand wet in the hallucinating rain

Ripped-off rolls, the crazy psychedelics
Wiped-off lines and the parallel stashes
Painting the world on a canvas with acrylics
The Reality of life lying as burnt ashes

Some find it amusing
Some find it comprehensive
A shift to the place where you can be happily pensive
Seeing everything in a single frame and still blankly gazing

Drags, snorts, puffs, and shots
Collided thoughts and shattered biases
Living your storylines again with everlasting plots
Living it up, not by breathing but by smoking pots

The Lust of Fame

The misty fog that blinded us all
The closest are visible, the farthest we see when everything fall
A clearer and wider perspective is what we all crave for
A cloak of distraction we all wore

When the waves come across the shore
We don't go all around wiping the seafloor
The right crime should be done at the right time
But who takes the call for what's the right time?

I fall on the verge of life being amusing or confusing
The contradiction to the fact that whether I'm hallucinating or breathing
The contractive mindsets that fall behind
The interior prime that we all were lured to find

Will it ever be achievable?
Will we ever be satisfied?
The fame, which is just a temporary label
Making our character more and more feeble

The Flawless Wink

The pen tames the paper with ink
Only then the emotions floating in the sea of heart can sink
All of this forces me to think
What damage can be caused with a single wink?

The instance when the heart takes over the mind
Even in solitude, peace becomes hard to find
Thinking all day and all for nothing
A bunch of celestial dreams, love brings

The Camouflaged Chaos

Chaos is what I have heard all my life
Like someone piercing my skin with a knife
Thought I was peaceful and the world was not
And so, on the grounds of mind, the battle for peace was fought

The perfect blacks and the perfect whites suddenly turned gray
Like cigarettes burnt out to ashes on an ashtray
I feel weak in my ability to think
Like a vessel sinking in water-filled to brink

The shallow path and the hollow heart
I fall short of the courage to walk
A painting made with tears as a form of art
My cluster of art about which I rarely talk

The Undesired Necromancy

The night's so silent or is it?
Did I hear screams or a hallucination it might be?
Paranormal, you call it, communication, it might be
The dead don't speak or is it?

The unattended knock on your door
The glasses shattered on your floor
The wooden chair that spontaneously sways
Experiences that you casually drift away

Some last wishes, some unfulfilled desires
Some unforgivable sins, some obligatory remorses
Some souls that never leave their corpses
Despite turning into ashes by fire

Ever felt a descent in temperature
Or an evil change in someone's nature
On a cold winter night, making the body sweat
The more you think, the scarier it gets

An Astrophile's Dream

And out there somewhere existed humanity
Where the people weren't insane
Beyond the horizons and across the lakes of salinity
Where the moments weren't mundane

Was it heaven or an illusion
Or was it just my mind's delusion
An endless time and space
Tying knots of infinity with its lace

A voyager in the orbit of perplexity
An astrophile by birth and blood
Polarizing the biases of parity
Like a light passing quasar without a single thud

The Girl in Blue Denim

The beauty of the blue sky lies short against yours
The wondrous smile that you gracefully hide against the lips of yours
The elegantly adorable threaded hair of yours
I have been of nobody else all my life, but yours

Every dress finds a pleasure when you wear it
Every aura of yours seems eternal, I swear it
It all seems tempting to be dreamt of
But the fact that you will never be mine, I fear it

The blue denim, the brown sweats
The gray top, the black flats
The white scarf and the golden earrings
A pleasure of a lifetime is what it brings

The silver lining of bracelet on your hand
If I were a cloud, it is all I want
The pearl ring that you wear like forever
An engravement on it is all I want

Quatrains

Dark clouds blending in with the glimmering city lights
Giving every eye a sense of delight
Passing on through the moment part of me still wonders
How blameless is the nature with its paradoxical blunders

True love as rare as it might seem
We see it as vivid as a lucid dream
And the search for it never ends
The firm belief in it never bends

The roads of success seemed lighted
Was it your perseverance or just an ardent desire?
Look at it now, the ashes cover the floor
All you are left with is a deceptive fire

Mediocrity is what I have feared all my life
And still have ended up being one of its kind
All that it has resulted in is just a mental strife

On the way to being exceptional, I've left the gaiety behind

The wall graffiti spilling the unsaid part
Wanna hear, you'll need an introspection
An outcast in the family of art
Ferrying the impressions, marks its redemption

Live for experiences, make memories
Give the world something to remember you by
Death is certain, life is borrowed at lease
Possess a heart whose kindness no one can deny

The beautiful eyes that the perceiver can't resist
The fall to which the smile is the actual jist
The hairs, the actions, and a lot more on the list
Guess what, today I've saw the true beauty in the abstract mist

Find me a poison I can't swallow
Darling, I walk and thunders follow
Not a preacher of light anymore
The cyclones don't scare me anymore

Holding my broken heart's pain
Lying on the canvas of love messed up with stain
Blisters and scars on skin removing your name
Hiding my tears, I cry in the rain

Cigarettes smell bad now
The love scars seem red now
Was it your ambience that made me fall
Once a dedicated lover, but now I hate it all

Smoke has always passed it all
My anxiety, sadness, and the unprecedented fall
Something I secretly love to hate it all
Something harder to leave and easier to call

The blue ink has shed tears of red
Emotions harder to control and feelings driving me mad
As if sensations I have felt were always sad
I tried to evade it all, but eventually its all what I get

The tragedy of life. I might have exaggerated it
Maybe for the world, I was a misfit
The warrior who always fled the battlefield
I always took cursing my luck as a shield

Roses are fine, but you are Red Camelia
Wines are toxic, but your eyes are the most addictive intoxication
As royal as the elegant princess of Illyria
If I was high for ever in life, you are my most ecstatic hallucination

Epilogue From The Pen That Spilled

The Wordplay was written with an intention of making the reader think, ally with musing ferried with an adhesive pun intended, either by making the reader question their biases or make them strong. The journey from the first word till the last sigh is a sinusoidal wave of emotions and introspection but the spinoffs with somewhat alternate notions are something that I have always liked personally and have been with my perception, adding value to it all along. I really hope that I was able to pass on them to the readers. Thank you for bearing with me!

9 798889 860570

Printed by Libri Plureos GmbH in Hamburg,
Germany